This Bo

MW01115517

Name:

Address:

Contact number:

Emergency Contact

Name:

Contact number:

Relationship to me:

A

Name	
Address	
Home	Work
Cell	Fax
Email	
Birthday	
Notes	

Name	
Address	
Home	Work
Cell	Fax
Email	
Birthday	
Notes	

Name	
Address	
Home	Work
Cell	Fax
Email	
Birthday	
Notes	

Name	
Address	
Home	Work
Cell	Fax
Email	
Birthday	
Notes	

Name	
Address	
Home	Work
Cell	Fax
Email	
Birthday	
Notes	

Name	
Address	
Home	Work
Cell	Fax
Email	
Birthday	
Notes	

A

Name	
Address	
Home	Work
Cell	Fax
Email	
Birthday	
Notes	

Name	
Address	
Home	Work
Cell	Fax
Email	
Birthday	
Notes	

Name	
Address	
Home	Work
Cell	Fax
Email	
Birthday	
Notes	

A

Name	
Address	
Home	Work
Cell	Fax
Email	
Birthday	
Notes	

Name	
Address	
Home	Work
Cell	Fax
Email	
Birthday	
Notes	

Name	
Address	
Home	Work
Cell	Fax
Email	
Birthday	
Notes	

B

Name	
Address	
Home	Work
Cell	Fax
Email	
Birthday	
Notes	

Name	
Address	
Home	Work
Cell	Fax
Email	
Birthday	
Notes	

Name	
Address	
Home	Work
Cell	Fax
Email	
Birthday	
Notes	

Name	
Address	
Home	Work
Cell	Fax
Email	
Birthday	
Notes	

Name	
Address	
Home	Work
Cell	Fax
Email	
Birthday	
Notes	

Name	
Address	
Home	Work
Cell	Fax
Email	
Birthday	
Notes	

B

Name	
Address	
Home	Work
Cell	Fax
Email	
Birthday	
Notes	

Name	
Address	
Home	Work
Cell	Fax
Email	
Birthday	
Notes	

Name	
Address	
Home	Work
Cell	Fax
Email	
Birthday	
Notes	

Name	
Address	
Home	Work
Cell	Fax
Email	
Birthday	
Notes	

Name	
Address	
Home	Work
Cell	Fax
Email	
Birthday	
Notes	

Name	
Address	
Home	Work
Cell	Fax
Email	
Birthday	
Notes	

Name	
Address	
Home	Work
Cell	Fax
Email	
Birthday	
Notes	

Name	
Address	
Home	Work
Cell	Fax
Email	
Birthday	
Notes	

Name	
Address	
Home	Work
Cell	Fax
Email	
Birthday	
Notes	

Name	
Address	
Home	Work
Cell	Fax
Email	
Birthday	
Notes	

Name	
Address	
Home	Work
Cell	Fax
Email	
Birthday	
Notes	

Name	
Address	
Home	Work
Cell	Fax
Email	
Birthday	
Notes	

C

Name	
Address	
Home	Work
Cell	Fax
Email	
Birthday	
Notes	

Name	
Address	
Home	Work
Cell	Fax
Email	
Birthday	
Notes	

Name	
Address	
Home	Work
Cell	Fax
Email	
Birthday	
Notes	

Name	
Address	
Home	Work
Cell	Fax
Email	
Birthday	
Notes	

Name	
Address	
Home	Work
Cell	Fax
Email	
Birthday	
Notes	

Name	
Address	
Home	Work
Cell	Fax
Email	
Birthday	
Notes	

D

Name	
Address	
Home	Work
Cell	Fax
Email	
Birthday	
Notes	

Name	
Address	
Home	Work
Cell	Fax
Email	
Birthday	
Notes	

Name	
Address	
Home	Work
Cell	Fax
Email	
Birthday	
Notes	

Name	
Address	
Home	Work
Cell	Fax
Email	
Birthday	
Notes	

Name	
Address	
Home	Work
Cell	Fax
Email	
Birthday	
Notes	

Name	
Address	
Home	Work
Cell	Fax
Email	
Birthday	
Notes	

D

Name	
Address	
Home	Work
Cell	Fax
Email	
Birthday	
Notes	

Name	
Address	
Home	Work
Cell	Fax
Email	
Birthday	
Notes	

Name	
Address	
Home	Work
Cell	Fax
Email	
Birthday	
Notes	

D

Name	
Address	
Home	Work
Cell	Fax
Email	
Birthday	
Notes	

Name	
Address	
Home	Work
Cell	Fax
Email	
Birthday	
Notes	

Name	
Address	
Home	Work
Cell	Fax
Email	
Birthday	
Notes	

E

Name	
Address	
Home	Work
Cell	Fax
Email	
Birthday	
Notes	

Name	
Address	
Home	Work
Cell	Fax
Email	
Birthday	
Notes	

Name	
Address	
Home	Work
Cell	Fax
Email	
Birthday	
Notes	

Name	
Address	
Home	Work
Cell	Fax
Email	
Birthday	
Notes	

Name	
Address	
Home	Work
Cell	Fax
Email	
Birthday	
Notes	

Name	
Address	
Home	Work
Cell	Fax
Email	
Birthday	
Notes	

E

Name	
Address	
Home	Work
Cell	Fax
Email	
Birthday	
Notes	

Name	
Address	
Home	Work
Cell	Fax
Email	
Birthday	
Notes	

Name	
Address	
Home	Work
Cell	Fax
Email	
Birthday	
Notes	

Name	
Address	
Home	Work
Cell	Fax
Email	
Birthday	
Notes	

Name	
Address	
Home	Work
Cell	Fax
Email	
Birthday	
Notes	

Name	
Address	
Home	Work
Cell	Fax
Email	
Birthday	
Notes	

F

Name	
Address	
Home	Work
Cell	Fax
Email	
Birthday	
Notes	

Name	
Address	
Home	Work
Cell	Fax
Email	
Birthday	
Notes	

Name	
Address	
Home	Work
Cell	Fax
Email	
Birthday	
Notes	

Name	
Address	
Home	Work
Cell	Fax
Email	
Birthday	
Notes	

Name	
Address	
Home	Work
Cell	Fax
Email	
Birthday	
Notes	

Name	
Address	
Home	Work
Cell	Fax
Email	
Birthday	
Notes	

F

Name	
Address	
Home	Work
Cell	Fax
Email	
Birthday	
Notes	

Name	
Address	
Home	Work
Cell	Fax
Email	
Birthday	
Notes	

Name	
Address	
Home	Work
Cell	Fax
Email	
Birthday	
Notes	

F

Name	
Address	
Home	Work
Cell	Fax
Email	
Birthday	
Notes	

Name	
Address	
Home	Work
Cell	Fax
Email	
Birthday	
Notes	

Name	
Address	
Home	Work
Cell	Fax
Email	
Birthday	
Notes	

G

Name	
Address	
Home	Work
Cell	Fax
Email	
Birthday	
Notes	

Name	
Address	
Home	Work
Cell	Fax
Email	
Birthday	
Notes	

Name	
Address	
Home	Work
Cell	Fax
Email	
Birthday	
Notes	

Name	
Address	
Home	Work
Cell	Fax
Email	
Birthday	
Notes	

Name	
Address	
Home	Work
Cell	Fax
Email	
Birthday	
Notes	

Name	
Address	
Home	Work
Cell	Fax
Email	
Birthday	
Notes	

G

Name	
Address	
Home	Work
Cell	Fax
Email	
Birthday	
Notes	

Name	
Address	
Home	Work
Cell	Fax
Email	
Birthday	
Notes	

Name	
Address	
Home	Work
Cell	Fax
Email	
Birthday	
Notes	

Name	
Address	
Home	Work
Cell	Fax
Email	
Birthday	
Notes	

Name	
Address	
Home	Work
Cell	Fax
Email	
Birthday	
Notes	

Name	
Address	
Home	Work
Cell	Fax
Email	
Birthday	
Notes	

H

Name	
Address	
Home	Work
Cell	Fax
Email	
Birthday	
Notes	

Name	
Address	
Home	Work
Cell	Fax
Email	
Birthday	
Notes	

Name	
Address	
Home	Work
Cell	Fax
Email	
Birthday	
Notes	

Name	
Address	
Home	Work
Cell	Fax
Email	
Birthday	
Notes	

Name	
Address	
Home	Work
Cell	Fax
Email	
Birthday	
Notes	

Name	
Address	
Home	Work
Cell	Fax
Email	
Birthday	
Notes	

Name	
Address	
Home	Work
Cell	Fax
Email	
Birthday	
Notes	

Name	
Address	
Home	Work
Cell	Fax
Email	
Birthday	
Notes	

Name	
Address	
Home	Work
Cell	Fax
Email	
Birthday	
Notes	

Name	
Address	
Home	Work
Cell	Fax
Email	
Birthday	
Notes	

Name	
Address	
Home	Work
Cell	Fax
Email	
Birthday	
Notes	

Name	
Address	
Home	Work
Cell	Fax
Email	
Birthday	
Notes	

Name	
Address	
Home	Work
Cell	Fax
Email	
Birthday	
Notes	

Name	
Address	
Home	Work
Cell	Fax
Email	
Birthday	
Notes	

Name	
Address	
Home	Work
Cell	Fax
Email	
Birthday	
Notes	

Name	
Address	
Home	Work
Cell	Fax
Email	
Birthday	
Notes	

Name	
Address	
Home	Work
Cell	Fax
Email	
Birthday	
Notes	

Name	
Address	
Home	Work
Cell	Fax
Email	
Birthday	
Notes	

I

Name	
Address	
Home	Work
Cell	Fax
Email	
Birthday	
Notes	

Name	
Address	
Home	Work
Cell	Fax
Email	
Birthday	
Notes	

Name	
Address	
Home	Work
Cell	Fax
Email	
Birthday	
Notes	

Name	
Address	
Home	Work
Cell	Fax
Email	
Birthday	
Notes	

Name	
Address	
Home	Work
Cell	Fax
Email	
Birthday	
Notes	

Name	
Address	
Home	Work
Cell	Fax
Email	
Birthday	
Notes	

J

Name	
Address	
Home	Work
Cell	Fax
Email	
Birthday	
Notes	

Name	
Address	
Home	Work
Cell	Fax
Email	
Birthday	
Notes	

Name	
Address	
Home	Work
Cell	Fax
Email	
Birthday	
Notes	

Name	
Address	
Home	Work
Cell	Fax
Email	
Birthday	
Notes	

Name	
Address	
Home	Work
Cell	Fax
Email	
Birthday	
Notes	

Name	
Address	
Home	Work
Cell	Fax
Email	
Birthday	
Notes	

Name	
Address	
Home	Work
Cell	Fax
Email	
Birthday	
Notes	

Name	
Address	
Home	Work
Cell	Fax
Email	
Birthday	
Notes	

Name	
Address	
Home	Work
Cell	Fax
Email	
Birthday	
Notes	

Name	
Address	
Home	Work
Cell	Fax
Email	
Birthday	
Notes	

Name	
Address	
Home	Work
Cell	Fax
Email	
Birthday	
Notes	

Name	
Address	
Home	Work
Cell	Fax
Email	
Birthday	
Notes	

K

Name	
Address	
Home	Work
Cell	Fax
Email	
Birthday	
Notes	

Name	
Address	
Home	Work
Cell	Fax
Email	
Birthday	
Notes	

Name	
Address	
Home	Work
Cell	Fax
Email	
Birthday	
Notes	

Name	
Address	
Home	Work
Cell	Fax
Email	
Birthday	
Notes	

Name	
Address	
Home	Work
Cell	Fax
Email	
Birthday	
Notes	

Name	
Address	
Home	Work
Cell	Fax
Email	
Birthday	
Notes	

K

Name	
Address	
Home	Work
Cell	Fax
Email	
Birthday	
Notes	

Name	
Address	
Home	Work
Cell	Fax
Email	
Birthday	
Notes	

Name	
Address	
Home	Work
Cell	Fax
Email	
Birthday	
Notes	

Name	
Address	
Home	Work
Cell	Fax
Email	
Birthday	
Notes	

Name	
Address	
Home	Work
Cell	Fax
Email	
Birthday	
Notes	

Name	
Address	
Home	Work
Cell	Fax
Email	
Birthday	
Notes	

L

Name	
Address	
Home	Work
Cell	Fax
Email	
Birthday	
Notes	

Name	
Address	
Home	Work
Cell	Fax
Email	
Birthday	
Notes	

Name	
Address	
Home	Work
Cell	Fax
Email	
Birthday	
Notes	

Name	
Address	
Home	Work
Cell	Fax
Email	
Birthday	
Notes	

Name	
Address	
Home	Work
Cell	Fax
Email	
Birthday	
Notes	

Name	
Address	
Home	Work
Cell	Fax
Email	
Birthday	
Notes	

L

Name	
Address	
Home	Work
Cell	Fax
Email	
Birthday	
Notes	

Name	
Address	
Home	Work
Cell	Fax
Email	
Birthday	
Notes	

Name	
Address	
Home	Work
Cell	Fax
Email	
Birthday	
Notes	

L

Name	
Address	
Home	Work
Cell	Fax
Email	
Birthday	
Notes	

Name	
Address	
Home	Work
Cell	Fax
Email	
Birthday	
Notes	

Name	
Address	
Home	Work
Cell	Fax
Email	
Birthday	
Notes	

M

Name	
Address	
Home	Work
Cell	Fax
Email	
Birthday	
Notes	

Name	
Address	
Home	Work
Cell	Fax
Email	
Birthday	
Notes	

Name	
Address	
Home	Work
Cell	Fax
Email	
Birthday	
Notes	

Name	
Address	
Home	Work
Cell	Fax
Email	
Birthday	
Notes	

Name	
Address	
Home	Work
Cell	Fax
Email	
Birthday	
Notes	

Name	
Address	
Home	Work
Cell	Fax
Email	
Birthday	
Notes	

M

Name	
Address	
Home	Work
Cell	Fax
Email	
Birthday	
Notes	

Name	
Address	
Home	Work
Cell	Fax
Email	
Birthday	
Notes	

Name	
Address	
Home	Work
Cell	Fax
Email	
Birthday	
Notes	

Name	
Address	
Home	Work
Cell	Fax
Email	
Birthday	
Notes	

Name	
Address	
Home	Work
Cell	Fax
Email	
Birthday	
Notes	

Name	
Address	
Home	Work
Cell	Fax
Email	
Birthday	
Notes	

N

Name	
Address	
Home	Work
Cell	Fax
Email	
Birthday	
Notes	

Name	
Address	
Home	Work
Cell	Fax
Email	
Birthday	
Notes	

Name	
Address	
Home	Work
Cell	Fax
Email	
Birthday	
Notes	

Name	
Address	
Home	Work
Cell	Fax
Email	
Birthday	
Notes	

Name	
Address	
Home	Work
Cell	Fax
Email	
Birthday	
Notes	

Name	
Address	
Home	Work
Cell	Fax
Email	
Birthday	
Notes	

N

Name	
Address	
Home	Work
Cell	Fax
Email	
Birthday	
Notes	

Name	
Address	
Home	Work
Cell	Fax
Email	
Birthday	
Notes	

Name	
Address	
Home	Work
Cell	Fax
Email	
Birthday	
Notes	

Name	
Address	
Home	Work
Cell	Fax
Email	
Birthday	
Notes	

Name	
Address	
Home	Work
Cell	Fax
Email	
Birthday	
Notes	

Name	
Address	
Home	Work
Cell	Fax
Email	
Birthday	
Notes	

O

Name	
Address	
Home	Work
Cell	Fax
Email	
Birthday	
Notes	

Name	
Address	
Home	Work
Cell	Fax
Email	
Birthday	
Notes	

Name	
Address	
Home	Work
Cell	Fax
Email	
Birthday	
Notes	

Name	
Address	
Home	Work
Cell	Fax
Email	
Birthday	
Notes	

Name	
Address	
Home	Work
Cell	Fax
Email	
Birthday	
Notes	

Name	
Address	
Home	Work
Cell	Fax
Email	
Birthday	
Notes	

Name	
Address	
Home	Work
Cell	Fax
Email	
Birthday	
Notes	

Name	
Address	
Home	Work
Cell	Fax
Email	
Birthday	
Notes	

Name	
Address	
Home	Work
Cell	Fax
Email	
Birthday	
Notes	

Name	
Address	
Home	Work
Cell	Fax
Email	
Birthday	
Notes	

Name	
Address	
Home	Work
Cell	Fax
Email	
Birthday	
Notes	

Name	
Address	
Home	Work
Cell	Fax
Email	
Birthday	
Notes	

P

Name	
Address	
Home	Work
Cell	Fax
Email	
Birthday	
Notes	

Name	
Address	
Home	Work
Cell	Fax
Email	
Birthday	
Notes	

Name	
Address	
Home	Work
Cell	Fax
Email	
Birthday	
Notes	

Name	
Address	
Home	Work
Cell	Fax
Email	
Birthday	
Notes	

Name	
Address	
Home	Work
Cell	Fax
Email	
Birthday	
Notes	

Name	
Address	
Home	Work
Cell	Fax
Email	
Birthday	
Notes	

P

Name	
Address	
Home	Work
Cell	Fax
Email	
Birthday	
Notes	

Name	
Address	
Home	Work
Cell	Fax
Email	
Birthday	
Notes	

Name	
Address	
Home	Work
Cell	Fax
Email	
Birthday	
Notes	

Name	
Address	
Home	Work
Cell	Fax
Email	
Birthday	
Notes	

Name	
Address	
Home	Work
Cell	Fax
Email	
Birthday	
Notes	

Name	
Address	
Home	Work
Cell	Fax
Email	
Birthday	
Notes	

Q

Name
Address

Home	Work
Cell	Fax

Email
Birthday
Notes

Name
Address

Home	Work
Cell	Fax

Email
Birthday
Notes

Name
Address

Home	Work
Cell	Fax

Email
Birthday
Notes

Name	
Address	
Home	Work
Cell	Fax
Email	
Birthday	
Notes	

Name	
Address	
Home	Work
Cell	Fax
Email	
Birthday	
Notes	

Name	
Address	
Home	Work
Cell	Fax
Email	
Birthday	
Notes	

Q

Name	
Address	
Home	Work
Cell	Fax
Email	
Birthday	
Notes	

Name	
Address	
Home	Work
Cell	Fax
Email	
Birthday	
Notes	

Name	
Address	
Home	Work
Cell	Fax
Email	
Birthday	
Notes	

Name	
Address	
Home	Work
Cell	Fax
Email	
Birthday	
Notes	

Name	
Address	
Home	Work
Cell	Fax
Email	
Birthday	
Notes	

Name	
Address	
Home	Work
Cell	Fax
Email	
Birthday	
Notes	

R

Name	
Address	
Home	Work
Cell	Fax
Email	
Birthday	
Notes	

Name	
Address	
Home	Work
Cell	Fax
Email	
Birthday	
Notes	

Name	
Address	
Home	Work
Cell	Fax
Email	
Birthday	
Notes	

Name	
Address	
Home	Work
Cell	Fax
Email	
Birthday	
Notes	

Name	
Address	
Home	Work
Cell	Fax
Email	
Birthday	
Notes	

Name	
Address	
Home	Work
Cell	Fax
Email	
Birthday	
Notes	

R

Name	
Address	
Home	Work
Cell	Fax
Email	
Birthday	
Notes	

Name	
Address	
Home	Work
Cell	Fax
Email	
Birthday	
Notes	

Name	
Address	
Home	Work
Cell	Fax
Email	
Birthday	
Notes	

Name	
Address	
Home	Work
Cell	Fax
Email	
Birthday	
Notes	

Name	
Address	
Home	Work
Cell	Fax
Email	
Birthday	
Notes	

Name	
Address	
Home	Work
Cell	Fax
Email	
Birthday	
Notes	

S

Name	
Address	
Home	Work
Cell	Fax
Email	
Birthday	
Notes	

Name	
Address	
Home	Work
Cell	Fax
Email	
Birthday	
Notes	

Name	
Address	
Home	Work
Cell	Fax
Email	
Birthday	
Notes	

Name	
Address	
Home	Work
Cell	Fax
Email	
Birthday	
Notes	

Name	
Address	
Home	Work
Cell	Fax
Email	
Birthday	
Notes	

Name	
Address	
Home	Work
Cell	Fax
Email	
Birthday	
Notes	

S	

Name	
Address	
Home	Work
Cell	Fax
Email	
Birthday	
Notes	

Name	
Address	
Home	Work
Cell	Fax
Email	
Birthday	
Notes	

Name	
Address	
Home	Work
Cell	Fax
Email	
Birthday	
Notes	

Name	
Address	
Home	Work
Cell	Fax
Email	
Birthday	
Notes	

Name	
Address	
Home	Work
Cell	Fax
Email	
Birthday	
Notes	

Name	
Address	
Home	Work
Cell	Fax
Email	
Birthday	
Notes	

T

Name	
Address	
Home	Work
Cell	Fax
Email	
Birthday	
Notes	

Name	
Address	
Home	Work
Cell	Fax
Email	
Birthday	
Notes	

Name	
Address	
Home	Work
Cell	Fax
Email	
Birthday	
Notes	

Name	
Address	
Home	Work
Cell	Fax
Email	
Birthday	
Notes	

Name	
Address	
Home	Work
Cell	Fax
Email	
Birthday	
Notes	

Name	
Address	
Home	Work
Cell	Fax
Email	
Birthday	
Notes	

T

Name	
Address	
Home	Work
Cell	Fax
Email	
Birthday	
Notes	

Name	
Address	
Home	Work
Cell	Fax
Email	
Birthday	
Notes	

Name	
Address	
Home	Work
Cell	Fax
Email	
Birthday	
Notes	

Name	
Address	
Home	Work
Cell	Fax
Email	
Birthday	
Notes	

Name	
Address	
Home	Work
Cell	Fax
Email	
Birthday	
Notes	

Name	
Address	
Home	Work
Cell	Fax
Email	
Birthday	
Notes	

U

Name	
Address	
Home	Work
Cell	Fax
Email	
Birthday	
Notes	

Name	
Address	
Home	Work
Cell	Fax
Email	
Birthday	
Notes	

Name	
Address	
Home	Work
Cell	Fax
Email	
Birthday	
Notes	

Name	
Address	
Home	Work
Cell	Fax
Email	
Birthday	
Notes	

Name	
Address	
Home	Work
Cell	Fax
Email	
Birthday	
Notes	

Name	
Address	
Home	Work
Cell	Fax
Email	
Birthday	
Notes	

U

Name	
Address	
Home	Work
Cell	Fax
Email	
Birthday	
Notes	

Name	
Address	
Home	Work
Cell	Fax
Email	
Birthday	
Notes	

Name	
Address	
Home	Work
Cell	Fax
Email	
Birthday	
Notes	

Name	
Address	
Home	Work
Cell	Fax
Email	
Birthday	
Notes	

Name	
Address	
Home	Work
Cell	Fax
Email	
Birthday	
Notes	

Name	
Address	
Home	Work
Cell	Fax
Email	
Birthday	
Notes	

V

Name	
Address	
Home	Work
Cell	Fax
Email	
Birthday	
Notes	

Name	
Address	
Home	Work
Cell	Fax
Email	
Birthday	
Notes	

Name	
Address	
Home	Work
Cell	Fax
Email	
Birthday	
Notes	

Name	
Address	
Home	Work
Cell	Fax
Email	
Birthday	
Notes	

Name	
Address	
Home	Work
Cell	Fax
Email	
Birthday	
Notes	

Name	
Address	
Home	Work
Cell	Fax
Email	
Birthday	
Notes	

V

Name	
Address	
Home	Work
Cell	Fax
Email	
Birthday	
Notes	

Name	
Address	
Home	Work
Cell	Fax
Email	
Birthday	
Notes	

Name	
Address	
Home	Work
Cell	Fax
Email	
Birthday	
Notes	

Name	
Address	
Home	Work
Cell	Fax
Email	
Birthday	
Notes	

Name	
Address	
Home	Work
Cell	Fax
Email	
Birthday	
Notes	

Name	
Address	
Home	Work
Cell	Fax
Email	
Birthday	
Notes	

W

Name	
Address	
Home	Work
Cell	Fax
Email	
Birthday	
Notes	

Name	
Address	
Home	Work
Cell	Fax
Email	
Birthday	
Notes	

Name	
Address	
Home	Work
Cell	Fax
Email	
Birthday	
Notes	

Name	
Address	
Home	Work
Cell	Fax
Email	
Birthday	
Notes	

Name	
Address	
Home	Work
Cell	Fax
Email	
Birthday	
Notes	

Name	
Address	
Home	Work
Cell	Fax
Email	
Birthday	
Notes	

W

Name	
Address	
Home	Work
Cell	Fax
Email	
Birthday	
Notes	

Name	
Address	
Home	Work
Cell	Fax
Email	
Birthday	
Notes	

Name	
Address	
Home	Work
Cell	Fax
Email	
Birthday	
Notes	

Name	
Address	
Home	Work
Cell	Fax
Email	
Birthday	
Notes	

Name	
Address	
Home	Work
Cell	Fax
Email	
Birthday	
Notes	

Name	
Address	
Home	Work
Cell	Fax
Email	
Birthday	
Notes	

X	

Name	
Address	
Home	Work
Cell	Fax
Email	
Birthday	
Notes	

Name	
Address	
Home	Work
Cell	Fax
Email	
Birthday	
Notes	

Name	
Address	
Home	Work
Cell	Fax
Email	
Birthday	
Notes	

X

Name
Address

Home	Work
Cell	Fax

Email
Birthday
Notes

Name
Address

Home	Work
Cell	Fax

Email
Birthday
Notes

Name
Address

Home	Work
Cell	Fax

Email
Birthday
Notes

X

Name	
Address	
Home	Work
Cell	Fax
Email	
Birthday	
Notes	

Name	
Address	
Home	Work
Cell	Fax
Email	
Birthday	
Notes	

Name	
Address	
Home	Work
Cell	Fax
Email	
Birthday	
Notes	

X

Name	
Address	
Home	Work
Cell	Fax
Email	
Birthday	
Notes	

Name	
Address	
Home	Work
Cell	Fax
Email	
Birthday	
Notes	

Name	
Address	
Home	Work
Cell	Fax
Email	
Birthday	
Notes	

Y

Name	
Address	
Home	Work
Cell	Fax
Email	
Birthday	
Notes	

Name	
Address	
Home	Work
Cell	Fax
Email	
Birthday	
Notes	

Name	
Address	
Home	Work
Cell	Fax
Email	
Birthday	
Notes	

Name	
Address	
Home	Work
Cell	Fax
Email	
Birthday	
Notes	

Name	
Address	
Home	Work
Cell	Fax
Email	
Birthday	
Notes	

Name	
Address	
Home	Work
Cell	Fax
Email	
Birthday	
Notes	

Y

Name	
Address	
Home	Work
Cell	Fax
Email	
Birthday	
Notes	

Name	
Address	
Home	Work
Cell	Fax
Email	
Birthday	
Notes	

Name	
Address	
Home	Work
Cell	Fax
Email	
Birthday	
Notes	

Name	
Address	
Home	Work
Cell	Fax
Email	
Birthday	
Notes	

Name	
Address	
Home	Work
Cell	Fax
Email	
Birthday	
Notes	

Name	
Address	
Home	Work
Cell	Fax
Email	
Birthday	
Notes	

Z

Name	
Address	
Home	Work
Cell	Fax
Email	
Birthday	
Notes	

Name	
Address	
Home	Work
Cell	Fax
Email	
Birthday	
Notes	

Name	
Address	
Home	Work
Cell	Fax
Email	
Birthday	
Notes	

Name	
Address	
Home	Work
Cell	Fax
Email	
Birthday	
Notes	

Name	
Address	
Home	Work
Cell	Fax
Email	
Birthday	
Notes	

Name	
Address	
Home	Work
Cell	Fax
Email	
Birthday	
Notes	

Z

Name	
Address	
Home	Work
Cell	Fax
Email	
Birthday	
Notes	

Name	
Address	
Home	Work
Cell	Fax
Email	
Birthday	
Notes	

Name	
Address	
Home	Work
Cell	Fax
Email	
Birthday	
Notes	

Name	
Address	
Home	Work
Cell	Fax
Email	
Birthday	
Notes	

Name	
Address	
Home	Work
Cell	Fax
Email	
Birthday	
Notes	

Name	
Address	
Home	Work
Cell	Fax
Email	
Birthday	
Notes	

Name	
Address	
Home	Work
Cell	Fax
Email	
Birthday	
Notes	

Name	
Address	
Home	Work
Cell	Fax
Email	
Birthday	
Notes	

Name	
Address	
Home	Work
Cell	Fax
Email	
Birthday	
Notes	

Name	
Address	
Home	Work
Cell	Fax
Email	
Birthday	
Notes	

Name	
Address	
Home	Work
Cell	Fax
Email	
Birthday	
Notes	

Name	
Address	
Home	Work
Cell	Fax
Email	
Birthday	
Notes	

Name	
Address	
Home	Work
Cell	Fax
Email	
Birthday	
Notes	

Name	
Address	
Home	Work
Cell	Fax
Email	
Birthday	
Notes	

Name	
Address	
Home	Work
Cell	Fax
Email	
Birthday	
Notes	

Name	
Address	
Home	Work
Cell	Fax
Email	
Birthday	
Notes	

Name	
Address	
Home	Work
Cell	Fax
Email	
Birthday	
Notes	

Name	
Address	
Home	Work
Cell	Fax
Email	
Birthday	
Notes	

NOTES